UNSEAMLY

Oren Safdie

BROADWAY PLAY PUBLISHING INC
224 E 62nd St, NY, NY 10065
www.broadwayplaypub.com
info@broadwayplaypub.com

Cover art by Sylvia Haber

First edition: September 2017
I S B N: 978-0-88145-730-8

Book design: Marie Donovan
Page make-up: Adobe InDesign
Typeface: Palatino

for Mia

ACKNOWLEDGMENTS

Thank you to Guy Sprung for taking a risk on this play (when others weren't), and being a staunch supporter of my work, and to Frances Hill for her commitment and resolve to bringing the play to New York. Much appreciation goes to The Blank Theatre, Canada Council for the Arts, Québec Government Office in New York, Holiday Inn in Coral Gables, Stephen Di Benedetto and the Department of Theatre at the University of Miami, Santa Monica Public Library, Susan Gurman, Daniaile Jarry, Ann Blanchard, Beth Hawke, Fritz Michel, MJ Kang, and of course, Shelagh McFadden.

UNSEAMLY was first produced by Infinithéâtre
(Guy Sprung, Artistic Director) in Montreal, Quebec,
opening in February 2014. The cast and creative
contributors were:

MALINA .... Arlen Aguayo Stewart
ADAM .... Howard Rosenstein
IRA .... Jonathan Silver

Directors .... Guy Sprung & Sarah C Carlsen
Set & costume design .... Cassandre Chattonier
Lighting design .... Cédric Delorme-Bouchard
Music composition & video design .... Nikita U
Choreography .... Amy Blackmore
Camera man .... Vladimir Cara
Assistant lighting designer .... Estelle Frenette-Vallière
Assistant stage manager .... Kate Hagemeyer
Stage manager .... Michael Panich

UNSEAMLY received its American premiere by Urban Stages Off-Broadway in New York City (Frances Hill, Producing Artistic Director; Peter Napolitano, Associate Producer) in October 2015. The cast and creative contributors were:

MALINA .... Gizel Jiminez
ADAM .... Tommy Schrider
IRA ....Jonathan Silver

Director .... Sarah C Carlsen
Set & costume design ....Brian Dudkiewicz
Lighting design ....Christina Watanabe
Sound design .... Douglas Mills
Choreography .... Gizel Jiminez
Projection design .... Nicholas Blade Guldner
Technical director & set construction.............. John Lavigne
Assistant stage manager .... Alexander Nixon
Stage manager .... Krystle Henninger

CHARACTERS & SETTING

MALINA, *20, an Hispanic, sexy, store manager.*
ADAM, *40s/50s, an off-kilter mid-level lawyer.*
IRA, *late 30s/early 40s, a dynamic C E O of a clothing company.*

Time: the present.

ACT ONE

Scene 1

(MALINA, 20, Hispanic, dark hair, sexy, sits in a lawyer's office, waiting anxiously. She could be already on stage while the audience is being seated.)

(ADAM, 39, a mid-level lawyer, emotionally suppressed, enters. He is dressed conservatively, and obviously on a tight budget.)

ADAM: Sorry to keep you waiting.

MALINA: That's okay. This office is very comfortable.

ADAM: Really… What about it gives you comfort?

MALINA: I don't know…the furniture, the wood…all those books.

ADAM: It's a laminant, you know.

MALINA: Excuse me?

ADAM: The wood paneling—all fake. (With resentment) Cheap plywood veneers stuck together with urea-formaldehyde, a known carcinogen, also used in the preservation of extracted human body parts… Does that change your view?

MALINA: (Not sure how to answer) Ah…

ADAM: Maybe I've just been working here too long.

MALINA: But the books are real.

ADAM: Of course…as is my degree.

MALINA: University of... *(Straining to read)* Pennsylvania?

ADAM: Pittsburgh. That old-fashioned typeface's a bit tricky—but I suppose it gives the whole thing a bit of legitimacy.

MALINA: That's near Pennsylvania, right?

ADAM: *(Taken aback.)* In Pennsylvania, correct.

MALINA: I'm from Southern California.

ADAM: *(This explains everything; condescending.)* Ah!... *(Reading off the file)* Malina...?

MALINA: *(As if she forgot to do it earlier, she jumps out of her seat and offers her hand.)* De Jesus, yes, sir.

ADAM: *(Standing up and shaking her hand, trying to bring it down to casual.)* Please, call me, Adam.

MALINA: I really appreciate you taking the time to meet with me...Adam.

ADAM: Yes, well, before we begin, I should let you know that the attorney who usually handles these matters is in court today. But I assure you that I am more than qualified to assess your complaint, as Labor & Employment was one of the two areas I articled in before settling on Mergers & Acquisitions. And when you get right down to it, aren't our co-workers consolidations of like-minded affiliates? ...The Boss, an appropriator of assets, seized by an insatiable appetite for domination?

(MALINA sort of half-smiles and nods her head in agreement—this metaphor going clearly over her head.)

ADAM: *(Bringing it back to basics.)* Won't you have a seat?

MALINA: *(Sitting.)* Thank you.

ADAM: Now...what can I do for you?

MALINA: Well, I'm not sure.

ADAM: If you're not sure, how do you think that makes me feel?

MALINA: I don't know.

ADAM: That was a rhetorical question.

MALINA: *(Feeling stupid)* Oh.

ADAM: Don't worry; my sense of humor is lost on a number of patrons. Why don't we begin with a few questions I pose to all potential clients.

MALINA: Okay.

ADAM: I pride myself on doing things a little different—focusing initially on emotional state before moving on to the facts. After all, what are facts void of context? It's like brushing your teeth without flossing.

MALINA: Oh, I floss.

ADAM: With wax?

MALINA: Yes.

ADAM: Best not—glides right over the plaque.

MALINA: I'll make a note of it.

(MALINA gets out a little pad, pen, and writes it down. ADAM just watches until she is finished.)

ADAM: So, how are you feeling?

MALINA: Right this second?

ADAM: Go for it.

MALINA: ...I don't really know how to put it into words.

ADAM: *(Leading her)* Could you be feeling someone has done you wrong?

MALINA: Yes.

ADAM: Taken advantage of you.

MALINA: Like so much.

ADAM: And now you're feeling ashamed.

MALINA: Exactly!

ADAM: Scared.

MALINA: No, not really—

ADAM: But intimidated.

MALINA: You mean—

ADAM: As to what the repercussions may be if you decide to go forward with this.

MALINA: I'm a lot stronger than most people think.

ADAM: I can see that.

MALINA: You can?

ADAM: Why else would you be here?

MALINA: Because I really want this bastard to—

ADAM: Now we're jumping ahead.

MALINA: Sorry.

ADAM: Don't worry; you're doing fine.

MALINA: I'm a bit nervous.

ADAM: *(To pacify her)* As am I.

MALINA: Really?

ADAM: To some extent ... So let me assure you that what's discussed between us today will be held in strict confidence; therefore it's imperative for you to be completely honest with me, even if you think it might contradi— *(Simplifying his language)* —go against your own interests.

MALINA: That makes me feel better.

ADAM: Good. Now I'm going to move on with a series of brief questions aimed at finding out the basic facts from which I'll determine whether it's in our interest to pursue this case further. Because as I'm sure you're aware, even though we offer this consultation service for free, time is still money.

MALINA: I totally understand.

ADAM: Incidentally, where did you hear about us?

MALINA: An ad on the Path train.

ADAM: I'm always amazed how much traffic that brings in. Was it the one with the gavel or the lawyers dressed up like cowboys?

MALINA: The gavel.

ADAM: Funny, I always thought the Wild West theme would be the eye catcher, but it hardly gets noticed.

MALINA: Maybe people think it's a T V show.

ADAM: Good point. I'll bring that up at our next meeting.

MALINA: *(Slightly paranoid.)* With who?

ADAM: The partners.

MALINA: Are you a partner?

ADAM: *(A sore spot)* Just about. *(Gets out a pad and paper)* ...Now, I'm writing these notes for myself, so it's not like a psychologist's office, where if I start scribbling it means I'm onto something.

MALINA: Okay.

ADAM: Have you ever been to one?

MALINA: What?

ADAM: A psychologist, therapist, or anyone of that nature.

MALINA: I started seeing a shrink three weeks ago.

ADAM: With what frequency?

MALINA: Five days a week.

ADAM: *(Digests this.)* And would it be safe to say that this may have been related to—or as a result of—trauma you experienced at work?

MALINA: I had a nervous breakdown the day after I left.

ADAM: *(While scribbling; encouraged.)* Perrr...fect.

(ADAM starts scribbling vigorously, and, MALINA—somewhat concerned—leans forward, trying to see what he's writing.)

ADAM: *(Without looking up; disciplining her)* Ah-ah!

(MALINA leans back in her chair.)

ADAM: Now, you mentioned to the secreta—*(Correcting his faux pas.)* administrative assistant that you felt you were sexually harassed, is that correct?

MALINA: Correct.

ADAM: Did the incident involve your employer or any other managerial position above you?

MALINA: He's the head of the company.

ADAM: Excellent. *(Checking off)* Did he ever make unfulfilled threats to impose a sexual quid pro quo?

MALINA: What does that mean?

ADAM: Did he offer you any sort of promotion or job security if you engaged in sexual relations with him?

MALINA: Definitely.

ADAM: Discuss sexual activities about himself or others in your presence?

MALINA: All the time.

ADAM: Off-color racist or sexist jokes?

MALINA: Both.

ADAM: Unnecessary touching?

MALINA: *(Don't get me started)* Oh my God!

ADAM: Commenting or speculating on your physical attributes?

MALINA: *(Becoming more emboldened and angry)* Does asking me about the shape of my vagina or whether my mouth is big enough to take him all in, count?

ADAM: *(Moving along)* Using demeaning or inappropriate terms, such as "Babe"?

MALINA: Try cunt, bitch, slut, whore, and guacamole penis pillow.

ADAM: Penis pillow?

MALINA: Like when a guy sticks his dick between a girl's breasts and jerks himself off?

ADAM: And the guacamole?

(MALINA's "don't you get it" look answers ADAM's question.)

ADAM: Right. *(Moving right along)* And finally…was there ever any kind of sexual encounter between you two?

MALINA: …Yes.

ADAM: Intercourse?

MALINA: Like everything you can imagine.

ADAM: And this was against your will?

MALINA: You see that's sort of where I get confused.

ADAM: Well, for example, did it happen on more than one occasion?

MALINA: Yes.

ADAM: Two…three times?

MALINA: A day at first, but then it trailed off to a few times a week.

(ADAM *looks up, astounded.*)

ADAM: Over a period of how long?

MALINA: Eight months.

(ADAM *stops writing and leans back, takes off his glasses and rubs his eyes.*)

ADAM: How long did you work for this company?

MALINA: Just over two years.

ADAM: And you're how old?

MALINA: Twenty.

ADAM: And when you started working there?

MALINA: Seventeen.

ADAM: *(Excited by this prospect)* Ah! So, this all took place while you were still a minor.

MALINA: Sort of…but not really.

ADAM: Can you be more specific.

MALINA: Like nothing fully-fully sexual or anything like that; but a lot of lead up, like when he whipped out his—

ADAM: *(Frustrated)* Again, please hold off on the details until I finish making my assessment.

MALINA: Sorry.

ADAM: *(Trying to hold it together)* It's okay, you're doing great… Now, does the company employ more than fifty people?

MALINA: Like thousands.

ADAM: Is it private or public?

MALINA: What does that mean?

ADAM: For instance, do they sell stock?

MALINA: Oh, right—he was totally obsessed with that—'cause like he had told his family to buy when it was really, really high, and then it went really, really low.

ADAM: What's the name of the company?

MALINA: The...   IRA: ...Standard

(Light shift: IRA SLATSKY, early 40s, somewhat scrawny but attractive, nervous energy, appears in the window and addresses the audience as if he's appearing on M S N B C's Squawk Box.)

IRA: ...is the fastest growing company in the history of this planet. While everyone else is farming their work out to sub-standard factories in Bangladesh and China, women and children slaving away twenty hours a day for a couple of cents, not even allowed to use the bathroom, we are the only sweatshop-free manufacturer set up in this country, that offers its workers a living wage, access to healthcare, and free massages—not to mention I personally take an interest in each and every one of my employees, offering interest-free loans, putting them up on my couch if they're wife throws them out—even gave one guy the shirt off my back after his house burnt down, so I don't know why you keep trying to rake me over the coals over such trivial matters; I'm one of the good guys!

(Light shift back to ADAM and MALINA. A weird smile comes over his face.)

MALINA: It's a clothing chain based in—

ADAM: Yeah, yeah, I know who they are. I don't think there's a lawyer in this country that doesn't. *(He gets up from his chair and paces back and forth, thinking.)*

MALINA: So you'll represent me?

ADAM: Well, you've been honest with me; so let me be honest with you.

MALINA: I'd appreciate that.

ADAM: The Standard, as I'm sure you're aware, is
famous for its sexualization of women. Their billboards
are a cross between *Barely Legal* and *Junior Scholastics*;
your boss, Ira Slatsky, has had his name splashed all
over the pages of every newspaper with numerous
sexual harassment allegations, and although none
of them have actually reached trial, let's just say it
seems money has changed hands. In addition, he's
openly bragged about pursuing relationships with
his employees and has a habit of pleasuring himself
in front of members of the press... Despite all this—
and much more—you still wanted to work for this
company and, in fact, became intimately involved with
him over a period of eight months. Yet somehow you
feel you've been taken advantage of. Please tell me
what I'm missing?

MALINA: It's hard to explain.

ADAM: Now would be a good time to make that
attempt.

MALINA: Like when you're in the middle of a dream,
and you know it's a dream, but you can't stop yourself
from doing what you're about to do because your body
is just too heavy and won't respond to your request
to wake up, but then when you finally open your eyes
and look around, you feel like in some ways the dream
was more real than life itself, which then makes you
realize that you never had control of your life in the
first place. Know what I mean?

(Sudden light shift)

*(IRA barrels out the door of his private office bathroom,
drying himself with a towel, wearing only a pair of pink
briefs, still dripping water. As he speaks—so fast, one
thought leading to the next, without stopping to breathe, like
he's loaded up on speed—he gets dressed, first pulling over a
t-shirt, then—later—pants.)*

IRA: ...Cock suckers—it was a fucking ambush—did you see what they did to me? Friggin' MSNBC. They don't fucking respect what we're trying to do here. Assholes don't recognize how we're revolutionizing the workforce. I have the highest-paid apparel workers in the Goddamn fucking universe? But they want to focus on some little off-the-cuff remark I made about my C F O— Know what I'm talking about?

MALINA: Sure.

IRA: I mean the guy's an incompetent fool, so why can't I say that? What are we in communist China—we have to pussyfoot around everyone's feelings? Truth is, they're all just jealous because they wish they could have my life instead of living in their tiny Brooklyn roach infested hovels, typing out that sensationalist shit. It's a fucking lynch mob mentality. My Goddamn relatives from Shtetl Poland didn't have to deal with such witch-hunts. *(Going up to her, showing her his underwear)* I mean, look at the stitching on this—show me another company that pays as much attention to detail and quality, and fucking made in the wham-bam-U S A!—not by some ingrain Paki who has to wash his clothes in some agent orange river, wife pregnant with a three-testicle kid. I mean, people leave these shirts in their will—they're so goddamn comfortable.

MALINA: I agree.

IRA: Of course you do. Or you wouldn't be working here. This is more than just a brand or a garment. It's a religion. History in the making. People empowerment. Industrial revolution. Do we sometimes push the boundaries of decency, dangle a little titty, twat and cock in their faces, try things that are a little "controversial"? Of course we do! It's hand-to-hand combat out there—everyone clawing for attention, trying to grab people's eyes from their sockets—and if we're going to survive against the A & F's, the F-c-u-k's, it ain't gonna be because of our high fucking morals. The ends justify our means—and you get that!

MALINA: Definitely.

IRA: *(Testing her)* What'd I just say?

MALINA: The ends justify your means.

IRA: That's what I'm looking for; a listener... What's your name again?

MALINA: Malina.

IRA: Right, De Jesus. You kind of caught me rushing here; my house is being treated for termites—fucking eating away at the roof, between the walls. Don't ever buy an old house before getting it inspected.

MALINA: I'll try and remember that.

IRA: You should see this place, it's the fucking Playboy mansion—but with class! Like some Romeo-Greek palace, crown moldings and shit—a dumb waiter to the kitchen—the fucking master bedroom is bigger than most people's houses. And it has five garages.

MALINA: Very cool; I love cars.

IRA: You like Mercedes-Benz?

MALINA: Are you kidding? That's like my ultimate dream to own one.

IRA: You got good taste. I have three of them. Maybe I'll let you take one out for a spin sometime.

MALINA: Really?

IRA: If you're a half-decent driver—why the fuck not.

MALINA: Oh, I'm a great driver. Never had an accident. No, that's a lie, but it really wasn't my fault 'cause like this guy opened his door right when I was pulling into a parking spot, and—

IRA: *(Not interested)* Right, right—so, what's your M O?

MALINA: Excuse me?

IRA: Your rap? Who's you is?

MALINA: You mean...

IRA: What makes you tick?

MALINA: Oh, well, many things.

IRA: I mean you seem like a smart chick and all, at least at first glance—I definitely sense that about you.

MALINA: Thank you.

IRA: Seem to have a desire to go places.

MALINA: *(Misinterpreting)* I would love to travel given the opportunity.

IRA: What are you, Mexican or Guatemalan or something?

MALINA: Dominican.

IRA: Oh, I love that—the mix. You know, kind of like half Spanish conquistador, half Pigmy—makes for an amazing ass. Know that part just between the back and where it starts to curve up—there's like this extra mini six pack of muscles—fucking spiritual—do you have that?

MALINA: I don't know.

IRA: That's why I use so many Latinas in my catalogue, 'cause, you know, it's the ass that counts. White girls are hit or miss—especially blonds. And Asians would be great, because I love those cheekbones...dark slanty eyes—totally hypnotic—but they got no booty. Like someone lopped it off, gave them a karate chop at birth. And when you get one with some cheek– maybe a Filipino, because she got some Hispanic blood passed down—she's like a fucking gold mine and knows it—kind of like a Jewish Princess without her daddy's

Amex—so she ain't gonna to do no catalogue unless you lay out four figures and you get down on your knees and beg for it...I mean, don't get me wrong, titties can sell too, but they've lost a lot of their cachet. Nobody knows what's real anymore, and don't kid yourself; the consumer picks up on that shit. Are yours real?

MALINA: What?

IRA: Your upper glands.

MALINA: Oh ... Sure.

IRA: Because they look terrific.

MALINA: A hundred percent silicone-free!

(IRA *stares lustfully after them; then catches himself.*)

IRA: *(Back to business-like.)* Anyway, tits have been done to death. Big, small, wide, flat with the large nipples, you know with big rubber erasers. I really love those, nice and dark, poking through a thin white cotton camisole, and not just when the wind blows, if you know what I mean. They really show up nicely in the black and whites. Next big thing I'm thinking about doing? ...Pubic hair!

MALINA: You mean like—

IRA: Big 80s jungle Afro-type—pouring out the thigh bands, none of this Brazilian bikini-wax shit. Let it all hang out—get some six-foot German Kraut with a blond muff, little curly cues under the arm pits, no deodorant, fucking crooked front teeth, now that's sexy—do you shave your pits?

MALINA: Um, yeah.

IRA: Why?

MALINA: I don't know.

IRA: Exactly!

(IRA *puts his hand up for a high-five.* MALINA *high-fives him back.*)

IRA: You're a fucking slave to popular culture, just like ninety-nine-point-nine percent of this goddamn world, like a flock of little bow sheep looking for their shepherd. What about your legs?

MALINA: Well—

IRA: You should try letting it grow, you know, just to try it out. Because it's all about doing what everyone else isn't. That's how you set a trend. Plus, it's totally natural. I mean you really think those cave women were sharpening rocks and carving up their shins in order to impress their cavemen? 'Course not. Form and purpose, Baby! Bodily hair holds in the warmth, diverts sweat, like those gutters and weeping holes in buildings. We're talking architecture. Product design. Now that's sexy... Mind if I take your picture?

MALINA: Umm...

(IRA *snaps a shot of* MALINA *with his iPhone before she knows what's hit her.*)

IRA: Turn.

(MALINA *does;* IRA *shoots.*)

IRA: I'm starting to photograph all my employees, thinking of maybe doing a spread featuring the people from the company—you know, keep it real, ethnic, local, that whole vertical integration thing. Yugoslavian Socialism. Would you be up for that?

MALINA: Definitely.

IRA: Lift your shirt up a bit—just to see some of your back.

(IRA *snaps, and shows* MALINA *from the screen.*)

IRA: See what I mean, you got that shit! *(Showing her the picture.)* I'm salivating... How old did you say you were?

MALINA: I'll be eighteen in a couple of months.

IRA: Fuck!

(IRA offers MALINA another high-five. She gives him another high-five.)

IRA: Seventeen... Now, isn't that the perfect fucking age or what? No cellulite, not a wrinkle, fresh skin— right at that stage in development that's like innocent little girl but starting to get into the naughty-slut stage... Missed out on all that when I was in high school: girl's didn't fucking give me the time of day. This one chick I dated for six months wouldn't even give me a hand job. Then, a week after we break up, she turns around and fucks half the chess club. Why do girls do that?

MALINA: I don't know.

IRA: Look where she is now—living in fucking Shigawake, with some lobster fisherman, probably scrounging to make a hundred bucks a day—what I earn in a fraction of a second. She only wishes she could suck my dick now.

(MALINA looks down. IRA leans forward; sincerely.)

IRA: I hope you don't mind me sharing this with you—I'm not trying to offend or show disrespect—just sharing my experiences as a way of explaining how you can take the negatives in life and turn them into positives.

MALINA: No, of course—

IRA: See, I always got hand me downs from my cousin when I was a kid. He'd go down to the States with his dad and bring back these perfect red tab Levi's—

because you couldn't get them in Canada—I mean, straight leg, shortened to perfection without losing the original cuff. But by the time they'd make their way to me, they were full of holes and rips—and that's before it was fashionable—whole thing made me look like some fucking squeegee boy. Mind if I snap a picture of your thigh—because we're thinking of getting into bikinis next summer.

(MALINA *raises her dress a little.*)

IRA: A little more?

(MALINA *complies.*)

IRA: It's like how can you not believe in God, Allah and Jesus Christ when you see that? And you're the perfect shade too. I mean imagine that skin color as a backdrop to like a really white guy's hand, long hairy knuckles, hovering above it… Right next to the seam of the bikini bottom. I mean it's *Blame It On Rio, Lolita* and *Jungle Fever* all in one. Can you picture it on a billboard in Times Square? Forget Calvin Klein. Every cab driver zipping down Broadway will be shooting his wad off, cars smashing right and left. I love it!… (*Motioning with his hand.*) Mind if I touch?

MALINA: If you have to.

(IRA's *about to touch* MALINA, *but then thinks twice and backs off as if someone else has yanked him away.*)

IRA: You must drive your boyfriend crazy with that shit.

MALINA: I don't have one.

IRA: (*To himself*) No fuck. (*His sits down in his "Captain's chair".*) What about an older brother?

MALINA: Just a sister.

(IRA *swivels around in his chair, looking at* MALINA. *We can almost see the wheels in his head turning.*)

IRA: Tell you what I'm going to do—because, unfortunately, we gotta wait until you turn eighteen— with the pictures. Fucking Brits took down one of my billboards last month 'cause they said the chick looked like some under-aged nymph faking orgasm, even though she was really a twenty-two year old stripper known for blowing more guys than Princess Diana in her chauffeur days. I mean you see what I'm up against? This fucking hypocritical puritanical society, like we're Victorians or something. And it's the Twenty fucking First Century. It drives me nuts… What happened to the constitution? Fucking First amendment! Freedom of expression! Magna Carta!… *(Calming down; getting really quiet, like he's crashed.)* But, hey, I shouldn't complain…I mean, look at me: business is on fire, I have more money than I know what to do with, a beautiful smart chick sitting in my office… Which store do you work in again?

MALINA: P C H.

IRA: *(Revved up again; on the move.)* Now that was one of my most brilliant moves—store's raking it in. You know, all those rich bitch Malibu teenagers with their noses in the air, cruising in daddy's B-mer, Platinum cards with unlimited credit, driving back from the city, maybe they've just been ditched by some homeboy 'cause they can't give decent head—and bam! They see the store with a picture of a chick on all fours, ready to take it up the pendejo, get a little gang-bang subliminal message going, or whatever sick fantasy they have, and it's like automatic: stock up on a few thongs, pink leggings, a skimpy T-shirt or two… Suddenly, they feel better about themselves. Know what I mean? You've seen that happen, right?

MALINA: All the time.

IRA: I'm a fucking healer.

MALINA: Yes you are.

IRA: A doctor of the mind, a shaman for the spirit,
that's what I am.

MALINA: Definitely.

IRA: Either that or they go home, chop off all their hair,
and turn themselves into fuckin' carpet-munchers—
which wouldn't be a half bad thing…I mean, I know
if I were a chick, I'd be lapping it up like some
abandoned kitten—talk about the earth's nectar:
someone should bottle that stuff—make an energy
drink out of that! …But now you got me off track: you
wanted to see me because…?

MALINA: Oh, well, I just wanted to tell you that I really
like- love what you do here. Even before I started
working at the store, I bought all my clothes at The
Standard. Like I have twenty T-shirts, and all my thong
underwear, and like I just think it's the greatest thing
ever, like, Apple computers, Ben & Jerry's or Google.
And like your fight for illegals and gays and all that,
workers' rights, it really speaks to me, you know, and
has made a deep impact on my life.

IRA: Are you legal?

MALINA: Of course.

IRA: Because you can level with me if you're not—
doesn't bother me. Just between you and me, half the
company's in the gray zone. I mean who else is going
to do that shit?

MALINA: No, no, I'm totally legal, my parents moved
here just before I was born.

IRA: Don't you just love that ? You're like this living
live fruit of the American dream. Parents sacrificing
everything for you—risking their lives, facing bullets,
barbed wire, deportation—just so you can have a better
life, like those ants that drown in the water to let their

brethren cross the river… And look at you now, you're
sitting in an office with one of the most successful C E
Os in the world. Amazing—this country. So, where do
you see yourself in five years?

MALINA: You mean, at this company?

IRA: If that's what you want.

MALINA: Oh, I don't know, I guess that's up to you.

IRA: Actually, it's up to you.

MALINA: Right.

IRA: But the fact that you persisted to get this
appointment—had the guts to come into my office,
and sit face to face with moi—shows me you've got
initiative right there.

MALINA: And I'm really a hard worker. I'm also
good with numbers, self-motivated, detail oriented,
extremely efficient—and I'll go high and beyond the
duties that this job requires.

IRA: I bet you will. How much are we paying you
anyway?

MALINA: Ten dollars an hour.

IRA: What, are you still in high-school or something?

MALINA: Just graduating. I've been saving money for
college. I want to major in Psychology.

IRA: College?

MALINA: Not that I'd have to stop working for you—
they offer night courses, and I can even minor in
Business!

IRA: Do you see any degree on this wall?

MALINA: No, but—

IRA: Fucking right, no. I'll tell you what you do see: a
profile in *The New Yorker*. Front page features in *The*

Times—both London and New York—and Los Angeles,
not to mention spreads in *Time, Newsweek, Vanity Fair,*
and I could go on and on—those are my bloody PhDs.
Nothing to do with Shakespeare or trigo-fucking-
calca-lunguemus…I mean, what do you think that
cousin of mine, with his Ivy League degree is doing
now? Fucking living with his family in a studio rent-
controlled shack—my uncle has to put him on the
payroll just so he can get health insurance—so don't
talk to me about college…

(Seeing MALINA *has cowered.)*

IRA: See, what I'm looking for is someone who's willing
to go that extra twenty miles—make this job their life…
and I sense you're the kind of girl who's right at a
tipping point—which you should read, by the way.

MALINA: *(Getting out a pen and marking it down)* Oh, I
definitely will.

IRA: Like, from this point on, your life can go in either
direction. You can study psychology, marry the first
guy who gives you a decent fucking orgasm, and have
three kids before he runs off with his dental hygienist,
or you can take another path, and become a force in the
fashion world, realize your full potential as a human
being, be in control of your own destiny. And let me
tell you something, it is a wild ride…and I'm only
getting started.

MALINA: *(With determination)* Look no further. I'm your
person. Really, I am!

IRA: You're sure.

MALINA: A hundred and ten percent!

IRA: Tell you what I'm going to do: that junior manager
in your store—the one with the cold sores?

MALINA: Evelyn?

IRA: Evelyn, right.

MALINA: They're white moles. She's really sweet.

IRA: And a fucking prude—wears extra wide pads under her leggings when she has her period—drives me nuts. Makes the clothes look like a pair of Pampers. I mean, why can't she just wear a tampon like everyone else?

MALINA: She has skin issues.

IRA: Well, then, don't wear the fuckin' leggings! Anyway, sales have been slagging lately—I've been thinking of moving her to Chinatown. Interested?

MALINA: In Chinatown?

IRA: Her position, fuck!

MALINA: Oh, I wouldn't want to take her job? We're good friends.

IRA: Okay, I don't have time for this. I have a shareholder's conference call in five minutes, I got an interview with C N N in half an hour, and you're worried about some fucking fifth rate manager's feelings?

MALINA: Okay, I'll do it.

IRA: That should take you up to twelve, plus it's a good way to get you some experience. Maybe ordering a few people around will toughen you up a little.

MALINA: Thank you, I totally appreciate it.

IRA: Don't let me down.

MALINA: Oh, I definitely won't.

IRA: Now, leave your cell number with my gal at the desk before you go in case I have to text you for some urgent reason.

MALINA: I don't get text messages.

IRA: Why the fuck not?

MALINA: *(Proudly)* Trying to be smart with my money.

IRA: Fucking, here… *(He takes out a couple of hundred dollars out of his pocket and throws it at her.)* If there's one thing I hate it's a cheapskate—shows that you have no confidence in yourself. Live beyond your means and you will live up to your potential.

MALINA: You're absolutely right; I'll do that from this point on.

IRA: Now, get the fuck out of here.

MALINA: Thank you so much.

IRA: Oh, wait; one more thing…

(MALINA turns around.)

IRA: *(He pulls a vibrator out of the box.)* Have any need for one of these?

MALINA: What is it?

IRA: Some sex shop in Milwaukee sent over a bunch as a token of appreciation—I donated a few hundred cock socks for an AIDS benefit. Suppose you can use them for just about anything. Unclogging drains, mixing cocktails—take one and think of me the next time you use it.

(IRA holds it out for MALINA; she hesitates.)

ADAM: And you took it?

MALINA: *(Coming back to her seat)* I didn't want to be rude.

ADAM: Use it?

MALINA: *(Uncomfortable)* Is that really important?

ADAM: Not to me… But that's just a taste of what kinds of questions they'll come after you with should you decide to go forward with this.

MALINA: ...I switched it on to see if it works.

ADAM: *(Coming right back at her)* For what purpose?

MALINA: Is this really necess—

ADAM: What did you use the vibrator for?

MALINA: *(Sheepishly)* Not to unclog my drain.

ADAM: Please be more specific.

MALINA: I had never used one before.

ADAM: You used it to pleasure yourself.

MALINA: ...Possibly.

ADAM: *(Pressing like he's the defendant)* While you were fantasizing of making love to Mister Slatsky!

MALINA: No way, he totally disgusts me!

ADAM: Then why didn't you quit right there on the spot?

MALINA: I needed the job.

ADAM: There weren't any others available?

MALINA: Not that paid as well.

ADAM: What was Gap offering?

MALINA: Nine twenty-five.

ADAM: So, for seventy-five cents an hour more, you were willing to forgo your dignity and swallow your pride.

MALINA: It adds up over time.

ADAM: So do the benefits of exercising, doesn't mean if you're obese with a heart condition you should go out and run a marathon!

MALINA: *(Taking it personally)* You think I'm fat?

(ADAM looks at MALINA, more out of pity than scorn, walks back to his desk.)

ADAM: *(Resigned; just for the formality)* Where do you work now?

MALINA: I'm still looking.

ADAM: How do you support yourself?

MALINA: Unemployment Insurance.

ADAM: And the shrink?

MALINA: It's pay as you can; she's in training.

(Beat)

ADAM: I'm sorry; I'm going to have to pass on this one.

MALINA: But—

ADAM: I wish you luck.

MALINA: I haven't even gotten to the part about—

ADAM: *(Motioning to the door)* I have other appointments.

(MALINA starts to walk out but returns for one last stand.)

MALINA: You know you really should change that ad on the train. You're actually just like all the other law firms.

ADAM: Ah, so you've approached others; I thought so. Well, here's a word of advice for the next sucker you bamboozle into wasting their time: when an attorney asks you to tell him the truth, it means the whole truth, and nothing but the truth. You can leave now. *(He goes to his file, inserts the paper and comes back, but she is still standing there.)* We're done.

MALINA: *(Mustering her nerve until finally, pleading with passion.)* If I told my friends I worked at The Gap or Abercrombie and Fitch, they'd laugh at me. But when I started working at The Standard, it was different. Suddenly, I was part of a cause—everyone wanted to know what it was like, friends begging me to get them clothes. It felt more than just some shitty job in retail—

even if it wasn't. The whole thing became a part of who
I was. My identity... And then when things started
getting crazy, I thought I could handle it. 'Cause if
everyone else working there is okay with it, then it
must be me, right? It shouldn't be such a big deal. After
all, how many thousands of women before me had to
spread their legs for some director to get the part; blow
their professor to get an A? ...But deep down, in my
gut, it wasn't okay. And then one day, my body no
longer cared what my mind was telling it, and I woke
up and... Here... *(She approaches him and holds out her
arm.)* Feel...

*(ADAM slowly takes MALINA's wrist in his hand. Feeling it
vibrate, he abruptly lets go.)*

*(ADAM sizes her up, his eyes widening as he realizes the
depth of MALINA's plight.)*

MALINA: I messed up—I know that. And if I could go
back and do things differently, I would... But I also
know that I'm a good person, and what he did to me...
(Becoming emotional) What he made me do to him....
What I had to.... *(She is crying; unable to speak.)*

ADAM: *(Moved by her; giving her a moment)* ...Okay, run
me through the events that followed your first meeting
with Slatsky leading up to the first sexual encounter.

MALINA: Thank you!

ADAM: Keeping it concise.

MALINA: Yes, well, after I got home from that meeting,
I was feeling really dirty, and just had to take a
shower—

ADAM: And sticking to the points relevant for our
purposes.

MALINA: Including my emotional state?

ADAM: Oh, no, we're way past that. Just the facts.

(Lights up on another area, with shelves and a box of clothes, suggesting a store. MALINA *starts folding the clothes from the box, and stacking them.)*

MALINA: Like Ira said, Evelyn was moved to Chinatown, and I got a raise. But I still had to do the same job because one of the managers from another store threatened to make a stink over seniority, or at least that's what he told me.

ADAM: So, he got in touch with you.

MALINA: There was a text message waiting in my inbox the minute my phone got hooked up.

ADAM: What did it say?

MALINA: He sent me copies of the photos he took of me. Plus he was curious to find out if I had had a chance to try out my "gift".

ADAM: The vibrator.

MALINA: Right.

ADAM: And he used that word?

MALINA: It was more in the form of a question, like a friend of his had experienced some problems with his drink mixer, and he wanted to make sure I was okay.

ADAM: What kind of problems?

MALINA: It gave off electric shocks.

ADAM: *(Personal curiosity)* Did you experience that?

MALINA: No.

ADAM: *(Back to business.)* And you text-ed him back?

MALINA: I didn't want to come off as rude.

ADAM: Might end up in Chinatown.

MALINA: Was that sarcastic?

ADAM: No.

MALINA: Because if you want me to trust you, I need to feel like I'm not going to be made fun of by my own attorney.

ADAM: *(Feigning deep regret)* You're absolutely right. Cheap Mergers & Acquisitions humor. It won't happen again. *(Jumping back into it mode.)* What was your reply?

MALINA: I thanked him for his concern, and told him that—... *(Seeing the damage now)* Can I just say, looking back at it now, I suppose if you try and twist it around, it can be made to look like I was okay with the whole thing, but underneath it was really really stressing me out.

ADAM: So you said. Did you share this with anyone else?

(MALINA looks down in shame. ADAM rubs his face—this is becoming more aggravating.)

ADAM: All right, all right, and then...

MALINA: He started texting me more, asking me all sorts of personal questions.

ADAM: Like what?

MALINA: You know, the basic stuff guys ask when they want to get to know you better.

ADAM: Humor me, please. I'm married seventeen years, have three children, and live in New Jersey. For all intents and purposes, I'm completely cut off from the youth culture of this nation—although next year my daughter turns twelve, which terrifies me to no end.

MALINA: Things like how many guys I've dated.

ADAM: How many?

MALINA: Five. Or whether I'd ever been with another woman—

ADAM: Sexually?

MALINA: Well, that's sort of what it means. Not necessarily full blown oral, or even second base, but kissing, feeling up, that sort of thing.

ADAM: *(Fascinated)* Really…

MALINA: And other male fantasy stuff, like did I like the taste of cum, or if I ever took part in a ménage.

ADAM: A trois?

MALINA: Like three or more. Pretty much what most guys in high school want to know when they're trying to get to know a girl.

ADAM: *(He seems shocked; more to himself.)* Maybe I need to consider home-schooling.

MALINA: Do you have any pictures?

ADAM: *(Taken off guard)* Of what?

MALINA: Your children.

ADAM: Yeah, sure. *(Almost without thinking about it, he whips out his wallet from his back pocket and flips it open, revealing a picture of his family.)*

MALINA: They're beautiful. *(Affectionately)* They have your eyes.

ADAM: *(Uncomfortable; pressing on)* So, throughout all this, you neither objected nor told him you felt uncomfortable in any sort of way?

MALINA: Again, in hindsight, I know it sounds creepy, but at the time, it just seemed to go along with the way the company operated. Plus…

ADAM: Yes?

MALINA: Well…

ADAM: Go on.

MALINA: There was also, like, a small part of me—the stronger part of me who refuses to be intimidated—that felt that, you know…

ADAM: No, I don't.

MALINA: Well, that I could…

ADAM: What?

MALINA: Empower myself to counter his power—but in a playful way that let him know who had the power.

ADAM: Showing him that you could compete on his level.

MALINA: Right.

ADAM: Take the sexual aspect off the table by bringing it fully into the open.

MALINA: Exactly.

ADAM: Even celebrating it.

MALINA: Like the way black people call each other nigga'.

ADAM: Got it…sort of… Okay, so, dildo—

MALINA: Vibrator.

ADAM: Right. Text messages, a little innocent get to know you back and forth verbal foreplay of what position you like, but also meant as a "I can play your game too," and—what happens next?

MALINA: Well, this is when I sort of feel it starts to cross the line.

ADAM: (A chuckle of irony escaping) Really?

(MALINA shoots him a look; he stops laughing in his tracks.)

MALINA: He invited me to accompany him to New York.

ADAM: (Encouraged) By text?

MALINA: Handwritten on a postcard—wanted to know if I would shadow him during Fashion Week. Thing is, when I turned the card over, there was a naked picture of himself.

ADAM: Do you still have it?

MALINA: Well, it wasn't really a picture as much as an old advertisement he had done for a gay magazine, which everyone had pretty much seen anyway.

ADAM: You don't have it.

MALINA: I mean, at the time, I just thought it went along with the humor of the company. When you have Penthouse centerfolds hanging in dressing rooms, and gay nude magazines at the check out counters, a little cap sticking out of the top of his boxers doesn't seem like anything out of the ordinary.

ADAM: *(Resigned)* You accepted his invitation.

MALINA: Fashion Week is like this really big deal, where you get to meet everyone who's anyone in the industry, and a lot of people from the company were going so, I mean, it wasn't like I was going to be alone with him, right? ...Plus it was my eighteenth birthday.

ADAM: You don't say.

MALINA: And, anyway, this was an opportunity to learn more about different aspects of the company.

ADAM: Which aspects are those?

MALINA: I mean he's hardly the first guy who wanted to fuck me.

ADAM: You just thought you could handle it.

MALINA: I mean, at first, he was being a real gentleman—introducing me to all these designers and retailers...explaining to me how the shirts were made and marketed... He even gave me a sneak preview into what the company was planning for the upcoming season.

ADAM: Must've felt like you had died and gone to Fashion Heaven.

(Off MALINA's disapproving look.)

ADAM: Sorry, more sarcasm. I apologize. Go on...

(MALINA gets up from the chair and starts undressing, staying in her underwear and putting on a thin, worn camisole. She gets into bed and holds a magazine in her hand.)

MALINA: But when I got back to my room that first night...there had been a change in the sleeping assignments. When I'd checked in that morning, I was sharing the room with two other girls, but suddenly they had been moved out, and the three single beds were replaced by a Queen size. At first, I assumed it was some kind of promotion, like he wanted me to feel like I was front office material.

(There's a knock on the door.)

MALINA: *(Startled)* Who is it?

IRA: Come on, open up, it's me.

(MALINA gets up, goes to answer the door in her underwear and camisole.)

MALINA: Is everything okay?

IRA: Yeah, it's just, I got my mother visiting, and I put her up in the company apartment, and she's with her boyfriend, and I get really unnerved whenever another man sleeps with her—even if they've been together for twenty-five years. I guess it just brings it all back, you know, all that stuff. Anyway, I tried to get another room, but the whole city's booked solid. So I was going to sleep in the park with the homeless people, you know, get their perspective on fashion trends—

but then I offered this bag lady some leftover shrimp cocktail, and she starts chasing me with a bat, and I thought to myself...well, you know, maybe...

MALINA: One second.

(MALINA *opens the door and* IRA *walks in.*)

ADAM: You let him in?!

MALINA: It was a different side to him. Like his ego had melted away, and all that was left was this really nice guy who seemed—

ADAM: Desperate?

MALINA: Misunderstood... And I mean, here's this famous multi-millionaire C E O of a world famous company, and he wants to share his deepest thoughts with me.

IRA: I understand if you're not comfortable with this. I mean, I'm not sure if I were you I'd let me in either... But all I want to do is crash. I promise, I'll keep all my clothes on.

MALINA: There's only one bed.

IRA: Don't worry; I'll take the floor. God knows how many nights I slept in my office when I was starting out... (*He goes into the bathroom, comes out with a couple of towels and starts making a bed on the floor. Noticing her; as if this is something he's been taught to ask.*) Did you do something to your hair?

MALINA: No.

IRA: Well, it looks really nice.

MALINA: Thanks.

(*Awkward moment;* IRA *lies down.*)

IRA: (*Relaxing*) Ahhhh...

MALINA: What?

IRA: You have this really calming effect on me.

MALINA: Me?

IRA: No one's ever told you that before?

MALINA: No.

IRA: You're still innocent—unpolluted by all the crap they spew out there—especially about me. They just want to find a target, string it up like a *piñata*, and keep bashing it 'till the guts pour out. Try and do something good for the people, and what do they write about? Some back-stabbing cunt looking to make a quick buck so she can kick back the rest of her life and bang her step-father. I mean calling a girl a slut can be an endearing term if it's said in the right context, don't you think?

(Off MALINA's *look)*

IRA: Sorry, I should've checked in with you to see if you're offended by this kind of talk—you might sue me too.

MALINA: Oh, you don't have to worry about that with me.

ADAM: *(Staunchly objecting)* Why not?

MALINA: *(Apologetic)* I wanted him to trust me.

IRA: I didn't think so. You're above all that, I can tell. I mean, why the fuck do people have to make such a big deal about sex anyway? If two people—who happen to work together—are attracted to each other, what's the big fucking deal? Know what I'm saying? If I fall in love at work, it's a beautiful thing, and that beauty should find expression. I mean, do you really think nature gave us these impulses in order for us to spend the rest of our lives suppressing them? Evolutionarily, it makes no sense. But I'm not telling you anything you don't know. Takes a lot more than a little dirty talk to

frazzle a girl like you. And if that's not enough, you're
like this beautiful sexy chick that probably has every
guy in your class whacking off to you right this second.

MALINA: *(Bashful)* I don't think so.

IRA: Is it even open for discussion?

MALINA: Does that mean you're still considering me
for a billboard?

IRA: Billboard? You don't want to be some brainless
bimbo—all skin and bones with that anorexic shit. Half
of them end up in Simi Valley shooting porn—eyes
glazed over like someone stuck a fist up their ass and
pulled out their souls. The only reason I use them is
because all the young girls today perpetuate some false
hedonistic myth about male preferences by sticking
their fingers down their throat after gorging on a half-
dozen Red Velvet cupcakes—I can't change that, at
least not yet—it's all about ends and means... Pay the
piper to feed the pauper. But if you're asking me what
a guy needs from a woman, give me some shank to
the bone, a little jiggle to wiggle... And you've got that
kind of beauty, like connoisseur class, or a fine wine;
with hips and an ass... No, no, you're too gorgeous
for all that shit—and smart—I saw that today with the
buyers. I mean do you really want your son surfing the
Internet twenty years from now, coming to you and
asking, "Mommy, why's that man's big toe poking up
your panties?" ...You're better than that.

MALINA: *(Touched.)* It's just my parents always talk
about how smart my older sister is 'cause she got like
straight As, and a scholarship to U S C in the sciences,
but with me it's always been, don't gain weight, Mali,
no man will want to marry you.

IRA: Fuck that shit. I mean what's your sister doing
now? Married to some dweeb, working in a lab
checking urine samples? Let me tell you something—

nobody thought I would amount to nothing. My own family wouldn't hire me to work in the back of their dress company. Even refused to back me on a loan with their bank. You got to fight those ghosts, prove your naysayers wrong.

MALINA: People don't really get the full picture of who you are, do they?

IRA: Don't get me wrong, there's a part of me—the pre-historic caveman side—that sometimes makes me—I wouldn't say objectify but, you know, distance myself emotionally...from women.

MALINA: That's too bad.

IRA: See, after my parents divorced, my mother joined this folk-rock group and was practically parading through the house with a different guy every night, not to mention my dad who got caught up in that whole Plato's Retreat group sex shit—but, hey, it was the 70s—wasn't their fault. Everybody was doing it... But that kind of stuff rubs off on you.

MALINA: Maybe that's why all your clothes are retro. *(Onto something)* Like there's a part of you that wants to go back in time and redo the past, return to the time when your parents were still together and you were a family.

(IRA looks at MALINA as like she doesn't now if he's going to hug or hit her.)

MALINA: I'm sorry, I didn't mean to—

IRA: *(Covering his vulnerability)* Hey, I'm an artist; a little suffering goes with the territory, right?

MALINA: It means a lot to me that you're sharing this with me.

IRA: *(Uncomfortable with the intimacy)* Hey, isn't your birthday coming up soon?

MALINA: *(Touched)* You remembered!

IRA: When exactly is it?

MALINA: Tomorrow.

IRA: Tomorrow?!

MALINA: Yes.

IRA: As in... *(Looking at his iPhone)* ...three minutes and twenty-one seconds tomorrow?

ADAM: *(Stepping in; to MALINA)* Can I just ask you one question?

MALINA: I'm not finished.

ADAM: But—

IRA: *(Quietly but forcefully; without looking at him.)* She said she's not finished.

ADAM: *(Stepping back out)* Sorry, my mistake.

IRA: That's amazing timing because I just happen to have your birthday present with me.

MALINA: Really!

ADAM: *(Sarcastic)* Really?

(IRA goes over to his bag and pulls out a beautiful new lace garment.)

IRA: Hot off the presses—it's my latest—Belgian lace, made in the U S A. Not even my creative directors have seen this one.

MALINA: *(Marveling)* Oh my God; it's stunning!

IRA: Why don't you try it on?

MALINA: Seriously?

IRA: Go for it.

MALINA: I wouldn't want to damage it.

IRA: Are you kidding me? You'll bring it to life.

(MALINA *is uncertain how to change.*)

IRA: You can change in the bathroom, if it makes you more comfortable.

(MALINA *takes the garment and goes into the bathroom to change.* ADAM *accompanies her into the bathroom but keeps it all business, looking straight into her eyes.*)

ADAM: I don't think I need to hear anymore.

MALINA: But this is when—

ADAM: Yeah, yeah, yeah... Look, I don't doubt that the events you've described are disturbing and emotionally traumatic, and there's no question that this guy is a jerk and probably won't change his ways until someone gives him a good beating, but it doesn't seem to me that you ever really asked him to stop. In fact, it could easily be argued that you encouraged him. I mean, for Christ's sake, you invited the guy to sleep in your hotel room—

MALINA: *(Taking off her dress)* I had no choice.

ADAM: On your eighteenth birthday! ...Can you imagine what the defense would do with this? There might even be a case to be made that you harassed him? And I haven't even gotten into the eight months.

MALINA: *(Handing* ADAM *her dress.)* Hold this for a second...

(ADAM *can't help but gawk at* MALINA'*s body, draped in nothing but her bra and underwear. One can almost hear his heart pounding. She grows impatient, and just slings her dress over his shoulder like he's a clothes hook, and slips into the lace garment.*)

ADAM: *(Trying to recover)* Maybe the best thing for you to do is chalk this up to one of life's hard lessons, because any girl who hangs around with a creep like this isn't going to get much sympathy from a jury. Lie down with a dog, chances are you're going to get—

(IRA *stands up and approaches the bathroom door.*)

IRA: Ready?

MALINA: *(Touching up her make-up)* Just about.

ADAM: I mean, did something traumatic happen to you when you were a child?

IRA: Because I'm going to huff and puff...

MALINA: Coming in a sec!

ADAM: Maybe some uncle or cousin tried to molest you?

IRA: Stop teasing.

MALINA: *(Directly to* ADAM*)* Do you love your daughter?

ADAM: I do.

MALINA: Let her crawl into your bed in the middle of the night and cuddle in your arms when she's afraid of the thunder?

ADAM: Of course.

IRA: This is cruel.

MALINA: Make sure she knows that no matter where you are or whatever you're doing, you will drop everything and come running to be by her side if she needs you?

ADAM: Absolutely.

IRA: Last chance.

MALINA: ...So did my father.

IRA: Meaning?

(MALINA *walks out the bathroom door, looking killer-sexy and smiles.*)

ADAM: Malina, wait! *(He watches the following helplessly—with the frailty of a father watching his own daughter.)*

IRA: *(Greeting her presence)* You are so friggin' hot.

MALINA: Thanks.

IRA: Eighteen years old.

MALINA: *(Excited but nervous.)* The big one-eight.

IRA: Old enough to do whatever you want.

MALINA: Free at last.

(IRA's back to the audience, he drops his pants…and isn't wearing any underwear.)

IRA: Happy fucking birthday.

(MALINA stares at his face, trying not to look down, somewhat shocked by the reality of what's happening.)

IRA: Well, aren't you going to blow out your candle?

(MALINA forces herself to get down on her knees and faces IRA's dick.)

IRA: How lucky are you…

(ADAM watches helplessly as MALINA takes a deep breath—as if "here it goes."—and starts to lean in.

END OF ACT ONE

(Light shift. Dance music comes on: something like Welcome to Saint Tropez. IRA *pulls* MALINA *up and they dance in a sexual manner. This continues for about thirty seconds, until the music abruptly cuts off, the lights shift back to the hotel room, and as they're coming out of a dance spin it turns into…)*

ACT TWO

Scene 1

(A couple of hours later in the same hotel room)

(IRA pulls MALINA by the hair away from the hotel door and throws her on the bed. He has a wild look in his eyes; she is terrified, trying to say and do anything to calm him down.)

IRA: *(Handing her a vibrator)* Now, take this wand and stick it up that tight juicy cunt of yours!

MALINA: Let me be…

IRA: Let you be? Are you hearing me all right, you fucking Chiquita banana? Because if you're talking, you can't be listening! Unless you're fucking deaf or something… Are you deaf?

MALINA: No.

IRA: Then what are you waiting for? Teasing me like some holier than art thou. Because I can walk out this door and have a thousand girls lined up with the snap of my fingers; really hot chicks who would die to be in your place right now.

MALINA: I know.

IRA: Then show me some respect! I'm Ira Slatsky— people admire me. Do you know what that means?

MALINA: *(Reciting as if she's had to learn it)* You have a large following. Intellectuals consult you. Major corporations seek your advice.

IRA: That's fucking right.

MALINA: Chicks bow to your dick when you walk into a room.

IRA: So, why aren't you bowing?

(MALINA bows several times in quick succession.)

IRA: Because you cannot come on this trip, have me introduce you to some of the most influential people in this business—and leave me high and dry. We're done when I say we're done, is that clear?

MALINA: Yes.

IRA: Then what are you waiting for?

MALINA: I really want to, it's just that I'm sore.

IRA: Damn right you're sore; I have nicks all over my dick from your fucking saber-tooth K-9s, but do you see me complaining? No pain, no gain—don't you know that? So grease up, baby, because we're only getting started.

MALINA: I know, maybe we can go out and get something to eat—to give us more energy.

IRA: You want energy? Part those lips; I'll give you
enough nourishment to last a lifetime. Instill you with
powers that you never knew you had...

(MALINA *starts heaving.*)

IRA: What are you doing?

MALINA: *(Gasping)* I need air. Can you open a window
or door? And then I'll masturbate for you in whatever
position you want. *(Falling apart; sobbing)* Please...just
give me some air, that's all I'm asking...

(MALINA *starts sobbing. This seems to shake* IRA *up.*)

IRA: *(Softening; the sensitive side)* All right, all right,
would you relax? I'm fucking crazy about you, don't
you now that? We got this amazing thing going ...
(Disengaging) But, hey, if this is too much for you, then
I'm not going to stand in your way... Go.

(IRA *steps away, opening a passage to the door.* MALINA
*slowly starts to test her freedom, inching over to her
suitcase, throwing her things in a bag, and running for the
door.*)

(IRA *jumps in front to block* MALINA.)

IRA: You are fucking going to lie back on that bed and
show me how your pussy loves this BOB, you hear me?

MALINA: Yes.

(*Resigned,* MALINA *takes the vibrator from* IRA, *goes back to
the bed, and lies down.*)

IRA: Start from the top and work your way down, nice
and slow. (*He takes a seat in a chair in front of the bed,
where he can get a full view, almost like he's watching a
movie. [Maybe he puts on his glasses.]*)

(MALINA *turns on the vibrator—low volume—and starts at
the top of her head, and very slowly works her way down. It
all seems mechanical, like she's bored.*)

(ADAM *kneels down next to the bed, almost like he's interviewing* MALINA, *and continues to question her with deep skepticism.*)

ADAM: …And you're saying this went on for eight hours.

MALINA: Yes.

ADAM: Straight through the night.

MALINA: That's how it happened.

ADAM: Not nine, not four, not six and a half—

MALINA: *(Definite)* Eight hours.

ADAM: How do you know? Did you time it?

MALINA: The sun was coming up when he left; he had an early meeting.

ADAM: And how many times during that period did you two… *(Having a hard time saying it)*

MALINA: Fuck? …Just once. He prefers to watch, then jerks himself off.

ADAM: …Oral?

MALINA: None on me. Twice on him… It was more for, like, the power or something.

ADAM: No breaks, no sleep, no food, didn't even let you go to the bathroom.

MALINA: Non-stop.

ADAM: Eight hours.

MALINA: Eight hours.

ADAM: That's a long time.

MALINA: Okay, maybe it was seven—does it really matter?

IRA: *(Coming back to the bedside, standing on the opposite side of* ADAM.*)* No, no, no, not like that. Do it like you mean it!

*(*IRA *takes the vibrator from* MALINA, *shifts it to a higher gear, hands it back to her, and returns to his chair.)*

*(*MALINA *starts to feign like she's getting into it, even as she answers* ADAM's *question quite factually—switching back and forth between the two realities.)*

ADAM: Because if you're saying he actually physically blocked you from leaving the room—

MALINA: That's right.

ADAM: Grabbed your arm—

MALINA: And wouldn't let go.

ADAM: In essence, held you hostage…

MALINA: I thought at one point he was going to kill me. *(Mock aroused by the vibrator—for* IRA*)* Ohhh.

ADAM: Then, that would constitute rape and kidnapping—both major criminal offenses. I mean this goes well beyond sexual harassment.

MALINA: *(Straight)* If that's what it is, that's what it was. *(Further aroused for* IRA's *benefit)* Ahhhh.

ADAM: But you never filed a report.

MALINA: I was afraid.

ADAM: Didn't tell management, a friend, maybe your sister? I mean, you could've even shot yourself an email.

MALINA: As I said, I really wasn't in a position to think straight. *(Aroused)* Ohhh God. *(Back to* ADAM*)* It's like I thought—

ADAM: This was normal behavior for the fashion industry—what you needed to do to get ahead.

MALINA: *(Looking directly at* ADAM; *aroused.)* Yes, yes, yes!

ADAM: *(Enticed by her; trying to fight it.)* S-s-so how long after this occurrence did you engage in further sexual acts with Slatsky?

MALINA: He forced me to blow him in the limo on the way to the airport.

ADAM: *(Astounded)* You got in a car with him the very next day?!

MALINA: Technically, it was two days, and how else was I supposed to get there?

ADAM: Ever hear of public transportation? ...A taxi? *(To himself)* Jesus... And after that?

MALINA: I kind of just did whatever he wanted.

ADAM: Why?

MALINA: I got promoted to manager! *(She jumps out of bed and walks over to The Standard store section, where she once again is arranging the clothes, but this time is more authoritative.)*

IRA: Come on, Ad-man, give me a break.

MALINA: *(Trying to be an ultra-sympathetic boss)* Tamara, do you think it's in any way possible for you to fold these shirts a little straighter? Thanks a bunch.

IRA: Don't tell me you believe any of this cockamamie shit?

MALINA: *(Calling out)* Helena, I know you went out drinking last night, but maybe you can keep bathroom breaks down to say three an hour? *Muchas gracias.*

*(*MALINA *checks out the leggings she's been folding, and decides she wants to try them on herself.* ADAM *watches as she seductively roles them up her legs, looks in the mirror, before taking them off and trying on another pair. She*

observes herself in the mirror, as if she's aware that a man she's trying to turn on is watching her.)

IRA: *(Coming up from behind him)* I mean, I know you're married and all, but remember how those bitches were when they started discovering their sexual power— the way those blossoming thirteen year-olds gussied themselves up for bar-mitzvahs, with those naughty cowboy boots, flipped bangs, knowing full-well that your hormones were doing 90 in a school zone ... So you fought back. Got yourself a couple of turntables, an amp, maybe some lights, and by the time Sweet 16s rolled around, you were the one in charge; a procession of young nubiles crowding around your table, begging for requests: *Stairway To Heaven, Suite, Clouds and Rain—*

ADAM: *(Remembering; song by Air Supply)* "I'm all out of love, I'm so lost without you."

IRA: You're in your quadruple seam Liberty Jeans—; shirt open with Bubby's Magen David bouncing up and down on your sprouting chest hairs, mike in hand, hand in air, and they're fucking hypnotized by you, waiting on every word as if you're the coming of the Messiah...

(MALINA starts swaying her hips in the mirror, loving how sexy she looks.)

ADAM: *(Longingly)* They wanted me...

IRA: And that's just a fraction of what I have to deal with on a daily basis. Fucking trailer trash bitches from Iowa texting me pictures of their vulvas. Pre-pubescent French chicks mailing me their creamed panties after they've had their first orgasm. It's a fucking jungle out there. And this girl, Malina, with that tan skin, long black hair, she's pure sex on a stick. The way that musky scent

(ADAM *breathes* MALINA *in.*)

IRA: snakes its way through your nostrils to your dick. And if you ever get a chance to see her without a shirt, your jaw won't just drop, it'll completely dislocate— because there are no words to describe flesh that defies gravity like that. *(Ira takes out a handkerchief and pats the sweat from Adam's forehead.)* And all this keeps coming at me like a 747 cruising to Bangkok with the jet stream at its back. At first I try to keep it professional, but she won't quit…

MALINA: *(Sexually suggestive; to* IRA*)* Wouldn't it be more practical for me to have my own room?

IRA: —she says to me after a shopping spree down Fifth Avenue courtesy of yours truly.

MALINA: After all, it's my birthday!

IRA: It doesn't take fucking Carnac to see what that implies…I mean have you seen the pictures of her?

ADAM: *(To* MALINA*; worried)* Pictures?

MALINA: *(Back to her straight self.)* The camera's practically attached to his wrist—keeps it with him twenty-four hours a day.

ADAM: What kind of pictures?

MALINA: They were meant to be used for an advertising spread across Europe.

IRA: You want spread? Get a load of this…

(IRA *calls up the pictures on his iPhone and shows them to* ADAM.*)*

ADAM: Full frontal nudity?

IRA: If you look closely you can see a little clit poking through.

MALINA: He said it would be airbrushed out.

IRA: *(Showing* ADAM*)* And this one…

ADAM: What kind of clothing could you possibly be selling with this?

MALINA: Nail polish.

ADAM: *(Looking closer; shocked)* Is that a string?

MALINA: They were pushing a new color called Menstruation.

IRA: I got dozens more.

ADAM: *(To* MALINA*)* And how exactly did you envision me explaining these photographs when they were introduced before a jury?

IRA: Damn right!

*(*IRA *comes over to* ADAM *and offers him a high five.* ADAM *obliges, but isn't quite sure why.)*

MALINA: It was all for work.

IRA: I mean, look at me, Adam. I'm no Killer Kowalski *(A professional wrestler)* —I can barely bench-press half my weight. *(Showing him a letter)* That bitch left the company without a complaint—even resigned with a letter of gratitude…

ADAM: *(To* MALINA*)* Gratitude?

MALINA: I had to sign it if I wanted to collect my last paycheck!

IRA: *(Putting his arm around Adam, taking him into his confidence.)* I think we both know what went down here…

*(*IRA *exits the motel room door,* MALINA *lies on the bed. Romantic music plays. He knocks on the door.)*

MALINA: *(Getting out of bed)* Who is it?

IRA: *(Low key, total change in character; concerned)* Hey, Malina, it's me. Open up.

(MALINA *walks to the door and opens it. Right away she is in high sexual gear.*)

IRA: Are you okay?

MALINA: Just fine.

IRA: I got here as soon as I could. Are you still feeling faint?

MALINA: It passed.

IRA: Glad to hear it. *(Turning to go)* I'll see you tomorrow—

MALINA: Wait!

(IRA *stops and turns.*)

MALINA: What time is it?

IRA: Ahh… *(Checking)* Almost midnight.

MALINA: *(Almost can't contain herself.)* Don't you know what that means?

IRA: It's way past my bedtime?

MALINA: It's my birthday!

IRA: *(Nonchalant)* Oh, right. Happy birthday. Sorry, I don't have a present for you—although, I got some new lace samples in the car if you'd like to try them on.

MALINA: That's okay. *(She approaches him, flirtatiously.)* Just you being here is the best present any girl can have… *(Trying to unzip him.)* Want me to suck you?

IRA: Whoa!… *(Stepping back; overly sincere)* You know, as much as I'd like to say yes, I don't think it's a good idea.

MALINA: Don't you find me attractive?

IRA: Of course I do.

MALINA: Because all I've been thinking about these past few months is what it might feel like to have all your genius sperm swimming inside of me.

IRA: That's kind of you to say, but I have a great deal of respect for you, Malina, and I think it would probably jeopardize our working relationship. Give it some time—you're still young, maybe a little impressionable—there's no need to rush into things.

MALINA: One kiss.

IRA: Malina—

MALINA: Just one kiss and I promise to leave you alone...after all it's my birthday.

IRA: Okay, but nothing more.

MALINA: *(Doing it very sexually)* Cross my heart.

IRA: *(For ADAM's benefit; looking over at him)* And you'll also stop sending me those dirty pictures of yourself masturbating on the toilet?

MALINA: *(Back to her own perspective; protesting to ADAM)* I swear I never did tha—

(IRA turns MALINA's head back around to face him and she returns to his vision of her.)

MALINA: I'll do my best, but it's really hard. I look at my body and see how sexy I am and just want you to have it.

IRA: I understand. As you know, I've wrestled with a few compulsions of my own. But I have a good therapist I can put you in touch with, which, of course, the company will pay for.

MALINA: You're such an amazing boss, like you should run for President or something.

IRA: *(To ADAM; off his skeptical look)* All right, maybe she didn't say that.

MALINA: So...my kiss?

IRA: On the cheek.

(MALINA *steps forward, turns* IRA's *head to face her—which he doesn't resist—and gives him a tender slow kiss on the lips... He momentarily pulls back.*)

IRA: *(To* ADAM*)* I mean, there's just so much a guy can take.

(MALINA *then goes into overdrive, pushing* IRA *onto the bed and starts unbuttoning his clothes, and kissing his chest.*)

ADAM: *(Taking a step toward the bed, observing them for a second.)* Reminds me of my first day of kindergarten...

(IRA *and* MALINA *stop momentarily, turn around, and give* ADAM *a quizzical look.*)

ADAM: My mother was late for work, so she had to drop me off at the curb. Luckily, a couple of First Graders were there, and assured her that they'd see that I got to my classroom. But as I watched her car pull away, I felt butterflies in my stomach and suddenly had to urinate. The two boys dutifully escorted me to the bathroom and, although I assured them I was capable of going by myself, accompanied me into the stall—to make sure I didn't hurt myself... When you're five years old, taking a leak isn't as simple as unzipping your fly and whipping it out—you pull your pants and underwear down to your ankles and lift up your shirt and hold it with your teeth so there won't be any mishaps... *(He shifts uncomfortably at the memory; swallows hard.)* ...The penetration of a crayon up my ass was a shock, but really wasn't that painful; it's the days that followed that kind of got to me: when you're scared to go to the bathroom 'cause you think all your insides are going to rush out. Still, I was determined to keep it a secret—humiliation being a key factor—until one morning my mother found some waxy blue residue on the seat of my Mickey Mouse pajamas—right between Mick's ears. Within hours, I was sitting in the Principal's office, along with

the two boys accompanied by their parents—one of
which happened to be the Principal herself—all staring
at me with such quizzical faces that even I started
to doubt my own story... Needless to say, nothing
came of it—oh, except in Second Grade; the two boys
cornered me in a parking lot, and beat the shit out of
me, chipped this tooth... The point being, everything
is subject to interpretation. And what finally emerges
as the "truth" is less a function of what actually
happens then it is about who holds the power...which
is probably what made me want to become a lawyer in
the first place... *(Walking back to his desk; disillusioned)*
Before I became one.

(Lights shift off the bed and onto the office as MALINA
chases ADAM back to his desk.

MALINA: *(Chasing after him and grabbing his hand and
spinning him around.)* You don't believe me!

ADAM: It's not important what I believe; if I take on a
client's case, it's because they believe, and I back that
belief a thousand percent.

MALINA: But I do believe.

ADAM: Of course you do—I don't doubt that—but
surely you can appreciate that without a witness,
not a single registered complaint, or any physical
evidence—except maybe a few provocative pictures...
of yourself!—it basically comes down to his word
against yours.

MALINA: Well, what about all those previous sexual
harassment cases filed against him?

ADAM: None of them went to trial.

MALINA: Because the women were paid off!

ADAM: In return for signing non-disclosure
agreements.

MALINA: I know for a fact that a lot of the girls working in the stores were paid money under the table to keep their mouths shut.

ADAM: Inadmissible.

MALINA: Then how about the way he's always going on to the press about sleeping with his employees?

ADAM: Reckless and deplorable, but not illegal in itself.

MALINA: So you're telling me that the head of a major company can say and do all these things and get away with it?!

ADAM: I'm saying that at this moment in time, with the evidence you've presented, I'm not in a position to advocate that this firm take on such a risk.

MALINA: *(Sensing something fishy)* Excuse me?

ADAM: My responsibilities at this law firm include insulating the partners from any potential negative repercussions.

MALINA: Are you saying I'm a negative?

ADAM: It's nothing personal.

MALINA: Because I doubt you'd be talking to me like this if I were some rich white girl living on Park Avenue.

ADAM: Now wait a minute—

MALINA: Doesn't justice mean anything to you people?

ADAM: Of course it does.

MALINA: Then why are you letting this creep get away with it?!

ADAM: There are guidelines to follow as to what we're permitted to take on, and this case does not meet that criteria.

MALINA: *(Reading into it)* So it's all about money.

ADAM: I hate to break it to you, but money is a factor in my line of business.

MALINA: Business?

ADAM: Profession. *(Pleading to her on a more personal level)* Look, if you really want to know, I've been busting my ass at this firm for the past ten years, doing sixty hour weeks, working every second weekend, covering for colleagues, and it just so happens that I'm coming up for review next month.

MALINA: What does that have to do with me?

ADAM: Meaning, if I don't make partner this time 'round, I'm basically on the street—just like you. And believe me, as far as the pecking order goes, I'm no pecker—I'm the peckee, competing against thousands of young attorneys fresh out of law school, willing to put in double my hours... So please try and understand what I'm up against here.

MALINA: Oh, so your boss brushes his leg against your crotch when he reaches over you to get his morning coffee?

ADAM: *(Looking down for second)* That's unnecessary—

MALINA: Tells you that if you bend over just a little more, he'll be in a better position to assess your future with the firm?

ADAM: *(Turning away from her)* I'm ending this conversation.

MALINA: But it's okay for you to pick apart my sex life.

ADAM: *(Right back at her)* You came to me.

MALINA: Exactly! So why aren't you helping?

ADAM: *(Frustrated with his powerlessness)* I can't!

(Pause)

MALINA: *(Disgusted by him)* You mean you won't. *(She gathers her things and starts to leave. Just before she's out the door…)*

ADAM: *(A matter of fact)* I'm leaving my wife.

MALINA: Excuse me?

ADAM: I haven't actually moved out yet, but I know it's coming: alimony, child support…all that fun stuff.

MALINA: *(Taking a step back in)* Maybe you should reconsider: studies show that people who divorce end up more unhappy than—

ADAM: It's beyond that.

MALINA: Because if you heard the way my parents argue—

ADAM: I'm on blood thinners—and I'm not even forty.

MALINA: Maybe you should try yoga—

ADAM: Meaning, my wife hasn't let me touch her in three years.

MALINA: Oh…

ADAM: What I'm trying to say is—

MALINA: No, no, I get it—

ADAM: If things were different—

MALINA: You'd consider taking me on.

ADAM: I put the odds at fifty/fifty. Without a retainer, this office operates on seventy/thirty. If you would've come to me a week or two later, but six months? I mean you haven't even laid out evidence that you were coerced to leave the company against your own will.

MALINA: Against my will?!

ADAM: Or in a manner that might be construed as hostile.

MALINA: *(A chuckle)* You mean like the time he woke me up in the middle of the night to pick up some Bulgarian model from the airport he told me he was planning on fucking.

(Lights up on the bed, where IRA *has been lying all along, but now he slowly comes back into the scene.)*

IRA: *(To* MALINA, *who doesn't acknowledge him)* I said, I wouldn't kick her out of bed—that's very different.

MALINA: Or how he invited me home for Thanksgiving, only to keep me cooped up in the hotel room answering phone calls?

IRA: I didn't feel our relationship was at a point where I felt comfortable introducing you to my family.

MALINA: Because I would've been fine if he left me alone. Just let me do my work as I always did. *(Turning to* IRA*)* But you couldn't let me be, could you? Showing up at my store with your new bitch, making me fit her in all the store's most expensive clothing. Ordering me to clean up her mess in the dressing room, while you two make out at the cash register.

IRA: It's a free country.

MALINA: *(Letting out all the hurt come out)* You wanted to humiliate me! And you knew I was powerless to do anything about it!!!

IRA: *(To* ADAM*)* You see what I had to deal with?

MALINA: *(Pushing through her tears; to* ADAM*)* And then out of nowhere—a few weeks later—I get this phone call from him, inviting me over for dinner.

IRA: Oh, you're not going to bring this up again.

MALINA: I show up, dressed all nice, thinking maybe he wants to make up, but instead there's this handicapped kid that opens the door. Mouth mangled, limbs twisted in every direction.

IRA: Poor kid was dragged half a mile under a bus when he was six years old.

MALINA: And I'm supposed to dance "sexy" for him.

IRA: Can you imagine what it must be like to be trapped in his body?

MALINA: "Lick your lips, show some leg, shake those titties, baby!"

IRA: I wanted to bring a little excitement to his life, is that such a crime?

MALINA: A few drinks later, a hit of speed, and he's reaching for my body. *(Disgusted)* Curled fingers trying to undo the buttons on my blouse.

IRA: *(Dismissing her claim)* Innocently brushed the back of his hand against your breast—happens every day on the subway.

MALINA: And when I look down, his zipper's open, and his dick is starting to poke through.

IRA: Okay, I admit I have no idea how he did that.

MALINA: Ira opens his wallet; starts throwing money at my feet: twenties, tens, fives, quarters.

IRA: I was just trying to create atmosphere.

MALINA: Cranks up the music, clapping his hands, and the whole room starts spinning.

IRA: *(His hand shielding his mouth; aside to ADAM)* Drunk as a skunk.

MALINA: Suddenly, I'm flat on my back down on the floor.

IRA: *(Trying to convince, ADAM)* Blitzed out of her gourd.

MALINA: And I feel something dripping…

IRA: It was drool, I swear it!

MALINA: Put my hand to my cheek, and it's sticky. It's fucking sticky!

IRA: Or maybe a booger, that's quite possible.

MALINA: So, I jump up, and by accident knock him in the face with my elbow—

IRA: Who the hell punches the handicap?

MALINA: Blood starting spewing everywhere.

IRA: She panicked.

MALINA: Starts making all these noises, like some wounded animal.

IRA: *(Giving her this)* I panicked.

MALINA: And Ira starts yelling at me: "What the fuck do you think you're—

IRA: *(In the moment of that scene; overlapping)* —...the fuck do you think you're doing to him?! You Goddamn crazy cunt? Don't you have any fucking brains?

MALINA: *(Feeling terrible; in the moment of the scene)* I was only trying to—

IRA: What? Knock off his head?!

MALINA: *(Feeling terrible about it.)* I'm sorry—

IRA: 'Cause let me tell you something, crooked limbs and all, he's fucking too good for you. You should only wish he wants to touch you! Now, get the fuck out of my house before I call the cops!

MALINA: I swear I didn't do it on purpose, I was only trying to—... *(Turning toward ADAM; calmly)* But, no, nothing you'd consider "hostile". *(She exits.)*

(ADAM spins around in his chair in frustration, throws a pencil across the room.)

IRA: *(Following MALINA to the door; continuing to yell at her after she's gone.)* And don't come back! Fucking wannabe. You were never interested in knowing who I am—just jump on the magic bus and go for a free ride like every other bitch! Truth is a girl like you is good for only one thing, and you weren't even good at that!... *(Stepping outside the door into the hallway)* And you should listen to your mother and get married before it's too late! Because a couple of years from now, you're ass is cottage cheese, and you're folding T-shirts at the GAP! ...In the warehouse!!!

(After a beat—almost as if IRA's *words have called* MALINA *into action—she's back, and more determined and confident than ever—ready to finish the job. She enters* ADAM's *office—with* IRA *on her tail—but shuts the door in his face.)*

*(*ADAM *turns around in his chair and sits up straight, relieved to see* MALINA.*)*

ADAM: Yes?

MALINA: *(As if she's bothering him)* I'm sorry.

ADAM: No, no—

MALINA: It's just—

ADAM: *(Inviting her to sit, with more enthusiasm)* Please...

MALINA: *(Taking a step in but not sitting)* I had a thought...

ADAM: Great.

MALINA: It might be completely out of line—

ADAM: Don't censor yourself.

MALINA: And please let me know if I'm overstepping my boundaries—

ADAM: Of course, of course—

MALINA: Because as you guessed, I've already been to a few other firms—

ADAM: *(Surmising)* You'd like a referral.

MALINA: No, no, I get it; I'm a risk. I have no money…
It's just that I was thinking—more like wondering—if
there might be any possible way for you to, like, in any
sort of way, sort of…you know…

ADAM: No, I don't.

MALINA: Coach me.

ADAM: What do you mean?

MALINA: Advise me, professionally, like you, alone,
yourself, as a lawyer on your own—outside of this
firm.

ADAM: That's impossible.

MALINA: *(Perhaps a hint of sexual connotation)* Of course,
I'd make it worth your time…pay you half of whatever
I'm awarded.

ADAM: It's not about the money. My contract strictly
prohibits me from taking on any outside work.

MALINA: You wouldn't have to put your name on any
documents if that's a concern.

ADAM: I even had to get permission to review my
mother's will.

MALINA: Then maybe just help me sort through some
of the paperwork.

ADAM: I wish it were that simple.

MALINA: *(Getting emotional)* Because I'm not going to be
able to move on with my life unless I see this through.

ADAM: I feel for you, Malina, I really do… But taking
on a company like this is a huge undertaking. It's not
something you can just file through small claims.

MALINA: *(Finding his eyes; making him see her
determination)* I'm willing to do whatever it takes.

(ADAM stares at MALINA, taken in by her zeal.)

(IRA *appears in the office window—after being shut out the door.*)

IRA: What're you waiting for? She's practically serving you her breasts on a plate.

ADAM: *(To MALINA; as if he's debating himself)* Thing is, it would be a really irresponsible thing for me to do, not to mention potentially jeopardize my career.

(IRA *hops through the window and snakes his way over to* ADAM.)

IRA: *(Coaxing him on)* On the other hand—

ADAM: —I have to be honest and tell you that this case fascinates me…a hell of a lot.

IRA: Nice…

ADAM: And when you walked out that door, a part of me felt like I had betrayed not only you, but myself… and the entire female species.

IRA: Let's not get carried away…

ADAM: Not that I want to give you false hope, because the obstacles to winning a case like this are enormous…

IRA: But—

ADAM: —perhaps once things settle down in my life, I'll be able to give you some sort of supplementary guidance.

MALINA: *(Exalted)* Really?

ADAM: A few hours a week should be manageable.

MALINA: Oh my God. I would be like so-so grateful— you have no idea!

ADAM: *(With a glance to the door; softly)* For obvious reasons, we wouldn't be able to meet on these premises.

IRA: Then where?

MALINA: I'd be more than happy to come over to your place—if that would make it easier…

(ADAM *hesitates, contemplates.* IRA *buzzes around him.*)

IRA: You don't have to justify yourself to me; I'd be worried if you behaved differently. I mean, maybe I have more charisma, money, fame, and get laid by dozens of hot girls more than you … But when you get down to it, we're just two guys looking for that extra edge, a couple of wild bucks, locking horns, trying to bag the biggest doe with the meanest set of loins. So stop fighting; you've earned it. Slaving away in this hole like some demented gerbil, going home to an ungrateful wife. It's a wonder you haven't blown your brains out yet… *(Starts to head back out the window)* And I hate to be break it to you, but when you're lying on your deathbed, a six inch catheter stuck up your ass, do you really think you'll be looking back on this moment and saying to yourself, you know I'm so glad I did the "honorable" thing?

MALINA: *(Sensing hesitation)* …Or we could meet at my place, if that's easier—my roommate stays with her boyfriend on weekends.

IRA: Moment of truth…

(ADAM *turns his attention to* IRA, *looks at him with disgust, and turns back to* MALINA *with renewed faith in his character.*)

ADAM: Weekends probably won't work, as it's the only time I'll get to spend with my children.

IRA: Think you're better than me?

ADAM: But I know of a coffee shop nearby where they pretty much leave you alone.

MALINA: Thank you so much. I'll be forever grateful for your kindness.

ADAM: Don't be; this is something I have to do for myself.

MALINA: And you really think you can prepare me to move forward with the case on my own?

ADAM: I don't see why not.

IRA: You're fooling—

(ADAM *goes to the window and pulls the shades down on* IRA, *effectively shutting him up—and out.*)

MALINA: I promise, I won't let you down. Whatever you need me to do, consider it done.

ADAM: I have complete confidence.

MALINA: And if it gives you any assurance, I'm willing to sign any agreement or contract that you feel is necessary.

(ADAM'*s face goes pale.*)

MALINA: In terms of sharing the money... For the work that you do...Adam? ...Are you okay?

ADAM: It's just...you didn't...

MALINA: *(Concerned)* What?

ADAM: Because I remember reading somewhere ... A law journal or maybe it was a fashion magazine ... something about Standard employees being forced to sign an agreement or some kind of contract, where by they agree to a provision that if any legal dispute arises for any reason whatsoever, the parties have to resolve the dispute through arbitration.

MALINA: Uh huh.

ADAM: In fact, if I remember correctly, the employee could be sued for a million dollars if he or she violated any part of the agreement.

MALINA: Right.

ADAM: Right, meaning you heard about it while you were working there, or right, you signed something similar to that effect?

MALINA: Well, I'd have to look over the papers more carefully, but it sounds kind of...familiar.

ADAM: Did you sign it or not?

MALINA: They make you sign a lot of things.

ADAM: Yes or no?

MALINA: *(Testing the waters)* Would it be a problem if I did?

(A weird, almost demonic, laugh comes out of ADAM.*)*

ADAM: Would it be a problem?

MALINA: That's what I'm asking.

ADAM: If signing such a clause would be a problem?

MALINA: Why do you keep repeating what I say?

ADAM: Putting your name on a piece of paper that says you forgo the right to sue. In effect, agreeing not to go public with any information about the company's practices, which is only the main weapon a prosecutor has going up against a company of this size, is that a problem? Taking away the ability to force a settlement—

MALINA: But I don't want to settle.

ADAM: *(Throwing his arms up)* And she doesn't want to settle!

MALINA: It was stupid of me, wasn't it? ...I knew it at the time...

ADAM: Of course you did.

MALINA: But it wasn't completely my fault.

ADAM: Of course it wasn't.

MALINA: It's just that...

ADAM: What?

MALINA: The thing is...

ADAM: Yes?

MALINA: But...

ADAM: What?

MALINA: But-but...

ADAM: What-what?

MALINA: I was only seventeen.

ADAM: *(Bingo)* Exactly!!!

(MALINA *stops crying and looks up.)*

MALINA: Huh?

ADAM: *(Energized like he hasn't been previously)* And desperate for work!

MALINA: Well, I was kind of desperate.

ADAM: Don't you see? Your signature on that piece of paper is our Holy Grail! The Hail Mary pass into the end zone with no time left on the clock, ball falling from the sky, arms stretched, fingers extended...feet just inside the line!

MALINA: And that's a good thing?

ADAM: It's better than good, Malina. It gives this case its meaning with a capital M... The kind that causes lawyers to swoon, giving them hope for eternal redemption.

MALINA: So you think this firm might—

ADAM: Malina, this firm won't only back you; they'll pull out every last stop. Call in every favor.

MALINA: But what happened to seventy/thirty?

ADAM: That's for a case; this is a cause! ...You were a minor when you signed that piece of paper, essentially strapping a muzzle over your mouth, forbidding you from telling the world your side of the story. But in this great country of ours, people don't stand for that! It only makes them want to know what's being hidden from them... And once information starts leaking out about this company's practices, the public won't stop demanding answers until every last stone is overturned.

MALINA: I thought nothing in the past counts.

ADAM: Not in a courtroom...but this is no longer about the law; it's about justice—the kind everyday people demand!

MALINA: The eight months?

ADAM: Could be two years for all anyone cares—once you violate a person's human rights, you've basically crossed into Jim Jones territory.

MALINA: Jim...?

ADAM: People's Temple? Massacre in Guyana? ... Convinced the entire parish to take their lives, murder their own children... It's hardly a stretch of the imagination to make the case that you were brainwashed—preventing you from seeing what was really going on. *(Giving her a contemporary references)* Like a Moslem stuffed into a Hijab. North Korea! Jaycee Dugard!! I mean, can anyone really blame her for not bolting out the door when her kidnapper left her alone?

MALINA: *(Protesting)* But that's what I was trying to tell you.

ADAM: Yes, of course you were, but you didn't frame it into a context... Don't you see, this is no longer about some sleazy boss trying to get it on with his employee, it's a cautionary tale about the times we live in, Sodom and Gomorrah, a test case for what our society is willing to put up with… You were told if you played your cards right, things would work out for you. But as it turns out, the deck was stacked against you, and if by some miraculous way you did win, the game you were playing never existed in the first place!

MALINA: *(Backtracking)* It's just I might've failed to mention that a few months after I quit, I asked for my job back.

ADAM: Irrelevant.

MALINA: Plus, Ira advanced me some money so I could put a deposit down on an apartment.

ADAM: A lovely gesture, I'm sure. But look what he has you turned into—it's the whole Stockholm syndrome—like some battered wife that defends her captor. Slatsky drew you in to the point that your free will has been compromised. Any decent therapist will see it that way—and we know just the right one that will… So?

MALINA: *(Suddenly afraid of the prospect)* I don't know.

ADAM: What do you mean, you don't know?

MALINA: It sounds complicated.

ADAM: Nothing could be simpler. *(Starting to seem a little like* IRA, *even in his mannerisms.)* We come out of the gate swinging; back him into a corner before he can even catch his breath. He says you're legally bound to keep silent? We yell so loud that the whole fucking universe hears us. Late Sunday night, we file the lawsuit on the East Coast. Monday morning—cue the music—we're on the *Today Show*. Push that whole hardworking immigrant story—

MALINA: My father was laid off.

ADAM: Even better! You were earning money for college.

MALINA: I was earning money for college.

ADAM: Of course you were; all I'm saying is we celebrate that. Put you in a business suit, maybe a pair of tortoise-rimmed glasses... Get your mother to release a statement to the press about your nervous breakdown?...

(Off MALINA's *disapproving look)*

ADAM: Or not... Because if we're going to take this guy on, we got to play by his rules—rip a page out of his playbook. Are you with me? *(He sees her non-answer as permission to continue.)* ...So Lauer comes on at seven, Slatsky's asleep on the West Coast—pitch black outside. He wakes up to a hundred phone messages—doesn't know what's hit him. Before he can go on the counterattack, we take out his favorite bullhorn: an exclusive with the Post, maybe give an interview with Coco Perez, and the whole mill takes over from there: C N N, Fox, M S N B C, they all follow. Then the Brits jump onboard—are you kidding? *The Mirror* will have triple orgasms for this shit!

MALINA: *(Revealing a potential penchant for the limelight.)* What about *The New York Times*?

ADAM: *(An inconvenient aside)* Forget them. With his legalize this, sweatshop-*free, that,* they'll turn you into a desperate cum junkie whore—*we* don't stand a chance... *(Continuing enthusiastically)* What's really important is that we roll out a number that boggles the mind—gives the every day Joe complete sticker shock—something like...two hundred and sixty million.

MALINA: Dollars!!!

ADAM: Because we don't just dump this on Slatsky—
no way—it's hardly a lone wolf operation. It's endemic
of the company's culture, which has been going
unchecked for years. So we include the entire Board
of Directors, closing their eyes to his shenanigans as
they went on collecting their six figure fees. *(With
resentment)* Let them go home to their trophy wives ·
and private school children, let them explain why
daddy's been going to bat for a sexual predator...
Suddenly, there's complete panic, everybody's running
to save their ass. *(As if he might help influence these
actions.)* Maybe some disgruntled worker smells blood
and jumps onboard with a discrimination lawsuit. An
accountant quits after he hears rumors that the S E C
wants to inspect the books; talk of an immigration raid;
impending bankruptcy; the stock starts to nosedive—

MALINA: *(Suddenly, enamored by the prospect of money)*
And that's when they offer me a settlement?

ADAM: Oh, no, they can't do that.

MALINA: *(Disappointed)* Why not?

ADAM: At least not yet... With everything they've
faced in the past, it would be nothing less than suicide.
An invitation to all those girls to come out of the closet
and claim their prize... No, no, you better believe
they're going to try and make an example of you—do
anything humanly possible to take you down. And
under normal circumstances, they might succeed... But
I'll bet my fee that any judge who takes one look at this
contract is going to tear it up and set a trial date.

MALINA: And if he doesn't?

ADAM: Worst case scenario, a year later our request
is denied, the case is sent to arbitration, I get my
wrists slapped by the Bar, and you get a few
hundred thousand to keep your mouth shut... More

importantly, Slatsky's reputation is obliterated, and if there's one thing we know for sure...

(IRA *bursts through the door, frantic, on his cell phone.*)

IRA: *(Freaked out)* What the fuuuuck!

ADAM: He cares deeply about his image—

IRA: *(Pacing back and forth)* I got my Goddamn grandmother calling, reading all this shit about me in her local paper—

ADAM: And he'll do whatever it takes to protect it—

IRA: —they're making me out to be some fucking rapist—

ADAM: With options running out—

IRA: —doesn't this bitch understand who she's dealing with?—

ADAM: —desperation will set in—

IRA: Go over to your computer—I'm shooting you a bunch of J-pegs—

MALINA: *(Horrified)* My pictures!

IRA: —I want you to blast the fuck out of them to every media source on this planet—

ADAM: —pictures that were taken for the express use of an advertising campaign—

IRA: —let the whole fucking world see how innocent she is—

ADAM: —that's invasion of privacy—

IRA: —head back, legs spread, fingers stroking that muff—

ADAM: —we file a second suit for ten million dollars—

IRA: —and one more thing—

ADAM: —if we really get lucky—

IRA: —register a new website in her name—call it "MalinaDe-Jesusphotos.com"—

ADAM: —that's fraudulent impersonation—

IRA: —but you got to make it look like something she's put together herself—

ADAM: —a criminal offense in California—

IRA: —using her own words—

ADAM: —meaning he can actually go to jail!

MALINA: But I don't want my breasts paraded all over the Internet.

IRA: *(In case she forgot)* And your vagina.

ADAM: Those pictures were supposed to be used on billboards anyway.

MALINA: For art.

IRA: Oh, no, baby, this will be pure porn.

ADAM: I understand the concern, and I'll do everything in my power to limit your exposure… *(Pleading)* But it's a risk we have to be willing to take.

IRA: *(Taking a different tact)* Listen to me, Malina…

ADAM: Don't you see, Malina…

IRA: *(Almost pleading)* We shared some crazy shit together—nobody can take that away from us—

ADAM: I've taken lemons and made you the best fucking lemonade lemons can make.

IRA: Was I a bit of a jerk at times?

ADAM: It's ingenious.

IRA: But you knew exactly who I was, and what you were getting into.

ADAM: Like Ness putting Capone away for tax evasion.

IRA: And if you think anyone's going to fall for that whole rape fantasy shit after you cleaned my clock for eight months straight, then someone's obviously been blowing a lot of steam up your pussy. *(He starts to go.)*

MALINA: *(Pointed)* That's the way you made me feel! It's how you make every girl feel when you walk into your stores, shoot them for an ad, tell them that if they play their cards right, there's no limit to how high they can climb!

IRA: So, this is about feelings? What about my feelings? How about the feelings of all the seamsters and cutters you'll be putting into jeopardy…shipping and receiving—thousands of decent hard-working people who came to this country with nothing but a little hope for the future, fix their teeth, send their kids to college… And if you think I'm just going to role over, and let you destroy this company then you obviously have no idea what I had to do to get where I am … I will fight tooth and nail for every last one of my workers even if it kills me!

MALINA: I was one of those workers too.

IRA: *(Mark my words)* You will go down. *(He exits.)*

MALINA: *(Her confidence evaporates)* Adam, I'm scared.

ADAM: *(Taking her hands; with conviction)* Don't worry, Malina, I promise I'll be right by your side, every step of the way, fighting for you as if you're my own daughter.

MALINA: *(Starts crying)* Because the thought of my parents seeing those pictures…

ADAM: I hear you, Malina, I really do.

MALINA: *(She buries her face into his chest.)* My sister will have a field day…

ADAM: Believe me, when this is over, and justice is served, she'll be so jealous of how proud your parents are of you…not to mention the millions of working women in this country who will see you as a beacon of hope, a Joan of Arc, drawing inspiration from your courage.

MALINA: *(Glancing up; inspired)* You really think so?

ADAM: I know so, Malina. This is historic. A "not-going-to-get-off-the-bus" moment.

(MALINA leans her head on ADAM's chest, and the two just stand in the middle of the room, holding each other, rocking back and forth slightly.)

MALINA: I can do this.

ADAM: Yes you can.

MALINA: I will do this.

ADAM: Yes you will.

MALINA: Nothing can stop me.

(ADAM and MALINA continue to embrace, but slowly his hand slides down her back, then to her butt. There is a frozen moment, not knowing where this will lead.)

ADAM: Tell me if I should stop…

(ADAM and MALINA remain frozen in an ambiguous hug as the lights slowly fade to black.)

END OF PLAY

www.ingramcontent.com/pod-product-compliance
Lightning Source LLC
Chambersburg PA
CBHW052210090426
42741CB00010B/2486